States

NEW JERSEY

by Jordan Mills

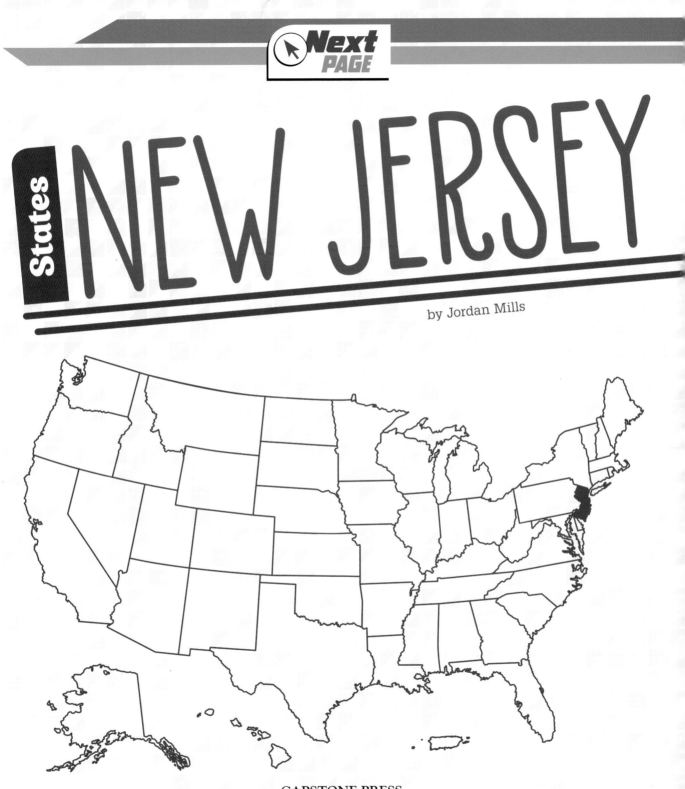

CAPSTONE PRESS
a capstone imprint

Next Page Books are published by Capstone Press,
1710 Roe Crest Drive, North Mankato, Minnesota 56003
www.mycapstone.com

Library of Congress Cataloging-in-Publication Data
Cataloging-in-publication information is on file with the Library of
Congress.
ISBN 978-1-5157-0417-1 (library binding)
ISBN 978-1-5157-0476-8 (paperback)
ISBN 978-1-5157-0528-4 (ebook PDF)

Editorial Credits
Jaclyn Jaycox, editor; Richard Korab and Katy LaVigne, designers;
Morgan Walters, media researcher; Tori Abraham, production specialist

Photo Credits
Capstone Press: Angi Gahler, map 4, 7; CriaImages.com: Jay Robert
Nash Collection, top 18, middle 18, bottom 18, top 19; Dreamstime:
Dejan Lazarevic, middle left 21; Getty Images: Museum of Science and
Industry, Chicago, 27; iStockphoto: nicoolay, 26; North Wind Picture
Archives, 12, 25; One Mile Up, Inc., flag, seal 23; Shutterstock: Andrew
F. Kazmierski, bottom left 8, bottom right 8, bddigitalimages, top
right 21, Blulz60, top left 21, Brad Camembert, bottom 19, Brian A
Jackson, 14, Chris Parypa Photography, 17, Christopher Penler, bottom
24, Daniel Prudek, bottom left 21, David Reilly, 16, Dawn J Benko, 7,
dcwcreations, 15, dinozzaver, top left 20, elinorb, bottom left 20, EQRoy,
9, Everett Historical, 28, f11photo, 10, gabriel12, top 24, Glynnis Jones,
29, Helga Esteb, middle 19, Jeff Feverston, bottom right 20, Jon Bilous,
cover, 6, Jorge Moro, 11, Kazakov Maksim, top right 20, R.Babakin, 5,
smereka, middle right 21, Steven Frame, 13

All design elements by Shutterstock

Printed and bound in China.
0316/CA21600187
012016   009436F16

TABLE OF CONTENTS

Want to take your research further? Ask your librarian if your school subscribes to PebbleGo Next. If so, when you see this helpful symbol 🖱 throughout the book, log onto www.pebblegonext.com for bonus downloads and information.

LOCATION

New Jersey is located along the Atlantic Ocean in the northeastern United States. To the south is Delaware Bay. The Delaware River runs along New Jersey's western border. Across the river to the west are Pennsylvania and Delaware. The Hudson River runs between New York State and northeastern New Jersey. New Jersey's only land border is on the north. It shares this border with New York. The largest cities are Newark, Jersey City, Paterson, Elizabeth, and Trenton, which is the state capital.

PebbleGo Next Bonus!
To print and label your own map, go to www.pebblegonext.com and search keywords:

NJ MAP

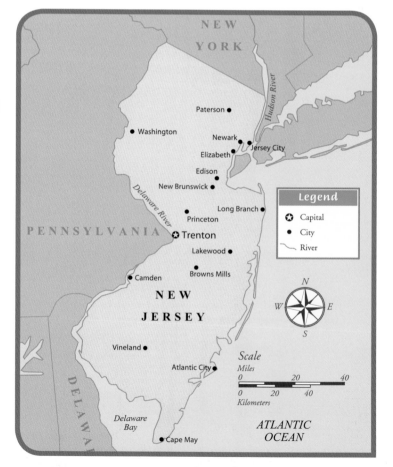

NEW YORK

Paterson ●

● Washington

Newark ●
Elizabeth ● ● Jersey City

Edison ●

New Brunswick ●

Hudson River

Delaware River

PENNSYLVANIA

Long Branch ●
Princeton ●
✪ Trenton

Lakewood ●

Browns Mills ●

● Camden

NEW JERSEY

Vineland ●

Atlantic City ●

Delaware Bay

● Cape May

DELAWARE

Legend
✪ Capital
● City
⌐ River

N
W   E
S

Scale
Miles
0   20   40
0   20   40
Kilometers

ATLANTIC OCEAN

4

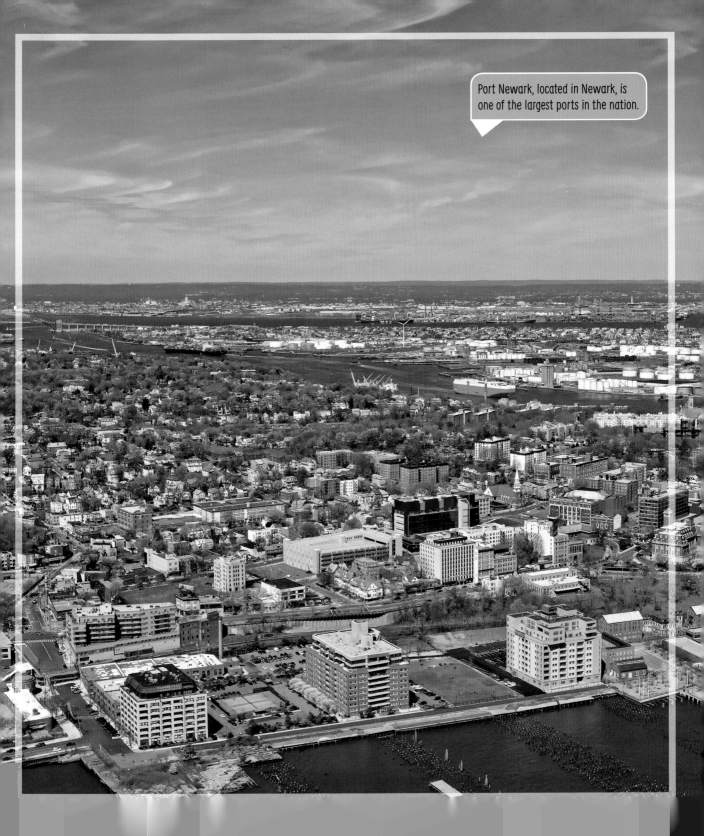

Port Newark, located in Newark, is one of the largest ports in the nation.

GEOGRAPHY

New Jersey has a variety of land features, including mountains, valleys, and beaches. The Kittatinny Mountains run along the northwestern border. The state's highest peak, High Point, is found in this area. It is 1,803 feet (550 meters) above sea level. The center of the state features mountains, forests, and rolling hills. The lowlands of the Atlantic Coastal Plain cover the southern three-fifths of the state.

PebbleGo Next Bonus! To watch a video about Cape May, go to www.pebblegonext.com and search keywords:

NJ VIDEO

The Delaware Water Gap National Recreation Area lies on the border of New Jersey and Pennsylvania. It covers 70,000 acres (28,000 hectares) and is used for hiking, fishing, canoeing, and other activities.

The Delaware River forms part of New Jersey's western border.

Legend

○ Area of Interest

▲ Highest Point

Mountain Range

River

High Point

Delaware Water Gap

APPALACHIAN RIDGE AND VALLEY

KITTATINNY MOUNTAINS

NEW ENGLAND UPLAND

PIEDMONT

Hackensack River

Hudson River

Passaic River

Raritan River

Delaware River

N W E S

ATLANTIC COASTAL PLAIN

Mullica River

Maurice River

Island Beach

Long Beach

ATLANTIC OCEAN

Delaware Bay

Scale

Miles

0   20   40

0   20   40

Kilometers

WEATHER

New Jersey has warm summers and cold winters. Summer temperatures average 70 degrees Fahrenheit (21 degrees Celsius) in the north and can be more than 85°F (29°C) in the south. Winter temperatures can fall to 24°F (-4°C) in the north and average 34°F (1°C) in the south.

Average High and Low Temperatures (Trenton, NJ)

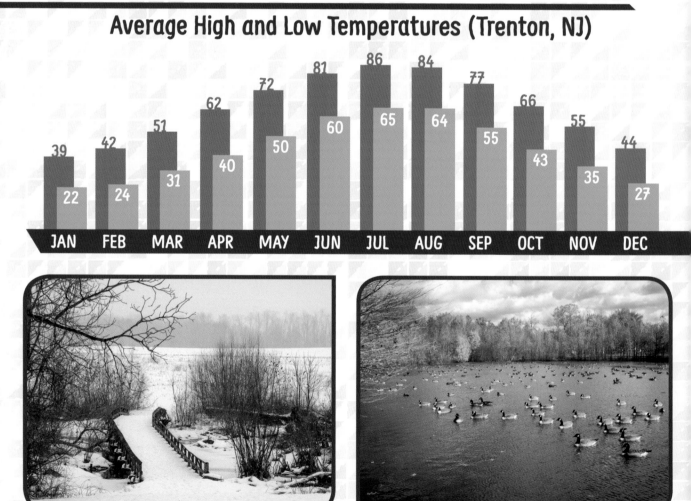

	JAN	FEB	MAR	APR	MAY	JUN	JUL	AUG	SEP	OCT	NOV	DEC
High	39	42	51	62	72	81	86	84	77	66	55	44
Low	22	24	31	40	50	60	65	64	55	43	35	27

Haddonfield

William Foulke discovered a dinosaur skeleton in Haddonfield, New Jersey, in 1858. This discovery launched the scientific study of dinosaur bones. Foulke's discovery, the *Hadrosaurus*, became the state dinosaur.

Atlantic City

This resort city in northeast New Jersey is known as the gambling capital of the East Coast. It is famous for its casinos and its boardwalk along the beach. It is traditionally the home of the Miss America Pageant. Street names in the board game Monopoly came from Atlantic City streets.

Great Falls

Great Falls is the second-highest waterfall east of the Mississippi River. Only Crabtree Falls in Virginia is higher.

HISTORY AND GOVERNMENT

Giovanni da Verrazano sailed to the West from France on the *Delfina*.

The first people to live in what is now New Jersey were likely ancestors of the Lenni Lenape. European explorers met them along the Delaware River in the 1500s. In 1524 Italian explorer Giovanni da Verrazano explored New Jersey's eastern coast. Dutch fur traders claimed land in this region in the early 1600s. English soldiers took control of the area in 1664. New Jersey became a royal colony in 1702.

During the Revolutionary War (1775–1783), New Jersey's location between New York City and Philadelphia made it a major battleground. In 1783 the colonies defeated Great Britain. On December 18, 1787, New Jersey became the third U.S. state.

New Jersey's state government has three branches. The governor leads the executive branch. The legislature consists of the 40-member Senate and the 80-member General Assembly. New Jersey's judicial branch has many courts.

The New Jersey state capitol building is the second-oldest capitol in the United States still being used today.

INDUSTRY

New Jersey is a highly industrialized state. Many factories are located in the Elizabeth - Jersey City - Newark area and in the Trenton - Camden area.

Chemicals are New Jersey's leading manufactured products. Prescription drugs are one of the most important types of chemicals made in the state. Other chemical products made in New Jersey include shampoo, perfume, detergents, and paint.

The headquarters for pharmaceutical companies like Johnson & Johnson and Merck are located in New Jersey.

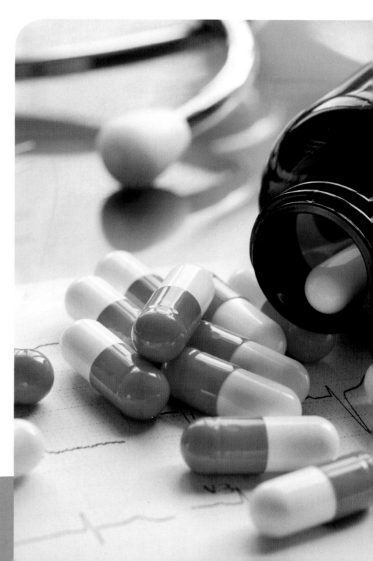

Although chemicals make up the largest percentage of manufactured products, New Jersey factories produce many other goods. Some companies make machinery, electrical goods, and clothing. Others print books and newspapers. Bakery goods, beverages, sugar products, and other processed foods also come from New Jersey.

The Campbell Soup Company's world headquarters is located in Camden.

POPULATION

New Jersey is the most densely populated state in the country. Most of New Jersey's residents live in the cities. The two largest ethnic groups in New Jersey are whites and Hispanics. The state's 6.1 million white residents include descendants of Italian, Irish, English, and German immigrants. New Jersey's Hispanic population includes more than 1.5 million people who came from places like Puerto Rico and Cuba. About 1.2 million African-American residents live in New Jersey. The state's Asian population includes more than 700,000 people.

Population by Ethnicity

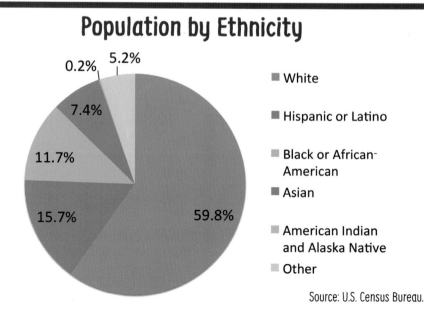

0.2%
5.2%
7.4%
11.7%
15.7%
59.8%

- White
- Hispanic or Latino
- Black or African-American
- Asian
- American Indian and Alaska Native
- Other

Source: U.S. Census Bureau.

FAMOUS PEOPLE

Grover Cleveland (1837–1908) served as the 22nd U.S. president (1885-1889) and as the 24th president (1893-1897). He was born in Caldwell.

Woodrow Wilson (1856–1924) was the 28th U.S. president (1913–1921). Born in Virginia, Wilson became president of Princeton University in 1902 and governor of New Jersey in 1910.

Thomas Edison (1847–1931) was one of the world's greatest inventors. He was born in Ohio and worked in New Jersey.

Albert Einstein (1879–1955) was possibly the world's greatest scientist. He is known for his theory of relativity, which deals with space and time. He was born in Germany and later moved to Princeton.

Bruce Springsteen (1949–) is a popular rock singer and songwriter. He performs with the E Street Band. He was born in Long Branch.

Judy Blume (1938–) is a writer. Her novels for children and adults have sold more than 80 million copies and have been translated into 31 languages. Her most popular works include *Are You There God? It's Me, Margaret*, *Superfudge*, and *Blubber*. She was born in Elizabeth.

STATE SYMBOLS

Tree

red oak

Flower

purple violet

Bird

eastern goldfinch

Fish

brook trout

Folk Dance

square dance

Shell

knobbed whelk

Dinosaur

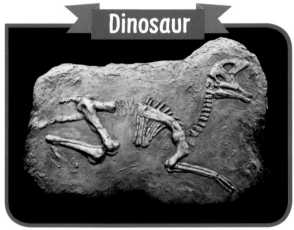

Hadrosaurus

Animal

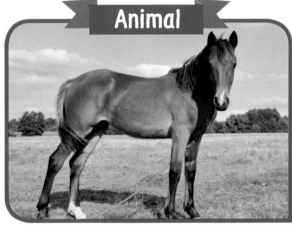

horse

Insect

honeybee

PebbleGo Next Bonus! To make a dessert using one of New Jersey's top-produced fruits, go to www.pebblegonext.com and search keywords:

NJ RECIPE

FAST FACTS

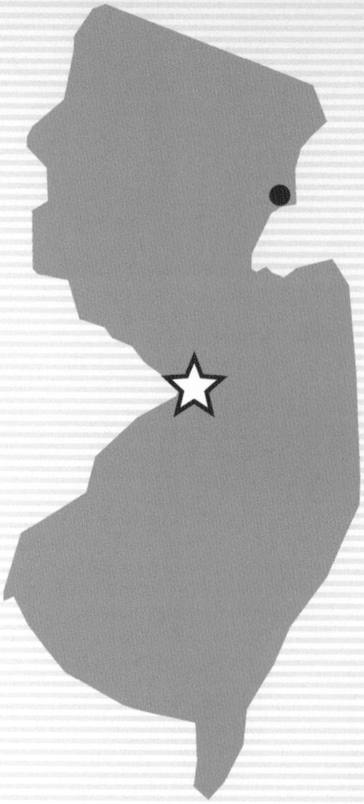

STATEHOOD
1787

CAPITAL ☆
Trenton

LARGEST CITY •
Newark

SIZE
7,354 square miles (19,047 square kilometers)
land area (2010 U.S. Census Bureau)

POPULATION
8,899,339 (2013 U.S. Census estimate)

STATE NICKNAME
Garden State

STATE MOTTO
"Liberty and Prosperity"

STATE SEAL

The New Jersey legislature adopted the original state seal in
1777. In the center of the seal, three plows on a shield represent
agriculture. A horse's head and a helmet appear above the shield.
The helmet represents the state's freedom from outside control.
A ribbon at the bottom includes New Jersey's motto, "Liberty and
Prosperity." It also includes the year of independence, 1776.

PebbleGo Next Bonus!
To print and color
your own flag, go to
www.pebblegonext.com
and search keywords:
NJ FLAG

STATE FLAG

The New Jersey state flag was officially adopted in 1896. The flag is yellow
with the state seal in the center. The seal has three plows with an armor
helmet and a horse's head above it. The helmet represents the state's
freedom from outside control. A ribbon at the bottom includes New Jersey's
motto, "Liberty and Prosperity." It also includes the year of independence,
1776. Two women represent the goddesses of Liberty and Agriculture.

MINING PRODUCTS

sand and gravel, traprock, granite, greensand marl, peat

MANUFACTURED GOODS

chemicals, computer and electronic equipment, food products, petroleum and coal products, fabricated metal products, machinery, plastics and rubber products, printed material

FARM PRODUCTS

flowers, shrubs, milk, peaches, blueberries, cranberries, tomatoes, corn, beans, potatoes, soybeans

PROFESSIONAL SPORTS TEAMS

New Jersey Gladiators (AFL)
MetroStars (MLS)
New Jersey Devils (NHL)

PebbleGo Next Bonus! To learn the lyrics to the state song, go to www.pebblegonext.com and search keywords:

NJ SONG

NEW JERSEY TIMELINE

1500s Lenni Lenape people live near the Delaware River in present-day New Jersey.

1524 Italian explorer Giovanni da Verrazano lands at Sandy Hook and explores the New Jersey coast.

1609 Henry Hudson explores Sandy Hook Bay and the Hudson River.

1620 The Pilgrims establish a colony in the New World in present-day Massachusetts.

 **1660** The Dutch settle in Bergen, the first permanent white settlement in New Jersey.

 **1664** Great Britain takes over New Jersey.

1702 East and West Jersey are united as one colony.

 **1776** The New Jersey colony adopts a constitution.

 **1787** New Jersey becomes the third U.S. state.

 **1825** John Stevens demonstrates the first U.S. railroad locomotive in Hoboken.

1861–1865 The Union and the Confederacy fight the Civil War. New Jersey fights for the Union.

 **1876** Inventor Thomas Edison opens his first laboratory in Menlo Park.

 1913 Woodrow Wilson, governor of New Jersey, becomes the 28th U.S. president.

1914–1918 World War I is fought; the United States enters the war in 1917.

1927 The Holland Tunnel connects Jersey City and New York City.

1937 The airship *Hindenburg* crashes at Lakehurst.

1939–1945 World War II is fought; the United States enters the war in 1941.

**1952** The New Jersey Turnpike opens, linking Philadelphia and New York City.

**1994** Christine Todd Whitman becomes New Jersey's first female governor.

2012 Hurricane Sandy strikes the Atlantic coast, causing more than 100 deaths and widespread damage, including extensive flooding.

2015 Historian Marina Rustow of Princeton University becomes a MacArthur Fellow.

Glossary

ancestor *(AN-ses-tuhr)*—a member of a person's family who lived a long time ago

descend *(dee-SEND)*—if you are descended from someone, you belong to a later generation of the same family

executive *(ig-ZE-kyuh-tiv)*—the branch of government that makes sure laws are followed

immigrant *(IM-uh-gruhnt)*—someone who comes from abroad to live permanently in a country

industry *(IN-duh-stree)*—a business which produces a product or provides a service

judicial *(joo-DISH-uhl)*—to do with the branch of government that explains and interprets the laws

legislature *(LEJ-iss-lay-chur)*—a group of elected officials who have the power to make or change laws for a country or state

locomotive *(loh-kuh-MOH-tiv)*—an engine used to push or pull railroad cars

novel *(NOV-uhl)*—a book that tells a long story about made-up people and events

tradition *(truh-DISH-uhn)*—a custom, idea, or belief passed down through time

Read More

Ganeri, Anita. *United States of America: A Benjamin Blog and His Inquisitive Dog Guide.* Country Guides. Chicago: Heinemann Raintree, 2015.

King, David C. *New Jersey.* It's My State! New York: Cavendish Square Publishing, 2015.

Meinking, Mary. *What's Great About New Jersey?* Our Great States. Minneapolis: Lerner Publications, 2016.

Internet Sites

FactHound offers a safe, fun way to find Internet sites related to this book. All of the sites on FactHound have been researched by our staff.

Here's all you do:

Visit *www.facthound.com*

Type in this code: 9781515704171

 Check out projects, games and lots more at
www.capstonekids.com

Critical Thinking Using the Common Core

1. What event occurred in New Jersey that launched the scientific study of dinosaur bones? (Key Ideas and Details)

2. What farm products does New Jersey produce? (Key Ideas and Details)

3. The first people to live in what is now New Jersey were likely ancestors of the Lenni Lenape. What is an ancestor? (Craft and Structure)

Index